Holy Sex
The Way God Intended

by
Michael Pearl

Published by
No Greater Joy Ministries, Inc.
1000 Pearl Road
Pleasantville, TN 37033
United States of America

Table of Contents

STOP!

This material is intended for mature audiences. Don't read this book unless you are married, have definite plans to be married in the next few weeks, or you are an older teenager whose parents have first read it and approve of you doing so.

If you don't think God meant for sex to be fun, this book is definitely for you.

Holy Sex

The Way God Intended

God did it!

The devil didn't create sex; God did. Sex is not the original sin; it is the original blessing. The first gift God gave to man was a beautiful, naked woman. The first commandment he gave them was, "Be fruitful and multiply," which means, "Copulate and make babies." After placing the naked couple together in the garden, their Creator looked upon them and said, **"Behold, it is very good."**

The Song of Songs

God gave the world a compilation of 66 individual books. Only one of those books majors on creation. One book contains psalms of praise. Another is full of wise proverbs. One majors on the deity of Christ, and just one book gives us the history of the early church. There is primarily one book that tells us about future things. And then there is one entire book of eight chapters that celebrates the beauty and passion of sex. It is frank, bold, lively, and absolutely blushless in its freedom and freshness.

Divine inspiration gave it the title, "Song of songs"–a rather high recommendation. It must have been at the top of the charts for a long time–a best-seller. That the ancient nation of Israel was comfortable including an erotic text in their Holy Scriptures reveals the difference in their attitude and that of this present culture. Unlike us, they had not surrendered the pleasures and art of lovemaking to the depraved and base elements of society. The righteous could talk about it, sing about it, attend a drama that encouraged marital love, and believe that "the way of a man with a maid" was a beautiful gift from God.

In this present age, where believers have accepted the cloud of shame cast over sex, the Bible still contains not just a discussion of sex, but a song to be sung in public, performed as a drama, presented at weddings, applauded in public, practiced at home—or, in the fields and forests.

Author

The events of our song begin in Jerusalem, move to the beautiful Sharon valley, then into the mountains of Lebanon, and back to Jerusalem. Solomon is identified as the husband. The woman of the song is his "**spouse**." She was married to him on the day his mother placed the king's crown on his head.

Apparently she was his first wife and the only love of his life. The bed on which they made love is identified as Solomon's. The first verse calls it Solomon's song. It could be that he wrote it, or it could be that it was written for him and, as such, is his song.

The man of the story was a shepherd and owned vineyards. His bride also tended sheep when she was young. Possibly Solomon was a shepherd before becoming king, or perhaps the song is written to make it generic and give it universal appeal.

Several details do not seem to fit an historical account of King Solomon and his wife. It is possible that the song is not intended as a literal account of their personal experience, but simply as a song about the average couple. The drama gives an account of the bride being beaten by night watchmen of the city. It is hardly likely that Solomon's wife ran through the streets searching for him and was abused by city employees. Furthermore, he returns from an extended stay in the mountains, where he had been shepherding, to seek his wife in a house where she is alone and the door is tied shut, as would have been the manner of securing the door on a common house. And in planning their lovemaking, she anticipates taking him to her mother's house; not what you would expect from King Solomon.

It seems that the song moves from the common to the kingly, making it the dream of the average shepherd. In reading the text, one can visualize two shepherds falling in love, marrying, making love outdoors, and then later ascending to share the magnificent bed in a king's palace.

The historical background is buried somewhere in antiquity. Though we can only guess at the facts surrounding this song, we do know that the Song of Solomon is as inspired by God as is the book of Psalms. One thing is for sure: the subject it so beautifully portrays is as powerful today as it was when written, and our present generation is much more in need of a sanctifying look at the most consuming passion God ever created.

Sensual

The song is primarily about her desires and feelings. She is represented as the initiator, pursuing him to draw him into her bed. She brags that his desire is toward her. She anoints her body with natural fragrances and spices and puts on jewelry to attract him. She is proud of her breasts and boasts that he was attracted to her because of them. She calls him an apple tree and dreams of eating his fruit. She dreams of him lying all night between her breasts, of the kisses of his mouth, of his embrace. When he says she is a garden enclosed, filled with fruit, she responds by inviting him to come into her garden and drink of her flowing juices.

The song speaks of senses excited by physical nature, fruit, birds, animals, springtime, sun, night, mountains, trees, and flowers. The reader is inundated with spices and odors, secret fountains, mountainous hideaways, and all this with allusions to their abandonment to erotic desires and experiences.

Everything he sees and experiences reminds him of the beauty and strength of her body. He sees her hips in the hips of a fiery horse, her torso in a strong tower, her hair in a flock of sheep, her breasts in a cluster of grapes, her arms and legs in the palm tree, her eyes in a turtledove, and hears her voice in the still night. He smells her breath in the apples, tastes her mouth in the honeycomb, sees her belly in a mound of golden wheat. When he drinks from a sealed fountain, he thinks of her purity and virginity. When any pleasant odor assails his nostrils, it reminds him of her—every herb, every spice, and every flower. His world is a crescendo of sensual experiences. It is often impossible to tell whether he is talking about the nectar from ripened fruit or the juices of her body. But in the end, he eats and drinks of the body of his wife and challenges the audience to do likewise.

Flesh and Spirit in Harmony

The religious world often views sex as the enemy of the spirit—the opposite of righteousness—as if the more you deny yourself, the more holy you are. But this inspired song reveals a worldview that is totally comfortable with enjoying the carnal and temporal in and of itself, and yet the sensual transports them onto a plane of spiritual experience that transcends the vehicle itself.

In this godly song there is no carnal versus spiritual; all of self is unified in the experience of marital love. The whole person—body and soul—is integrated with physical nature in perfect harmony

with everything without and within. It is only when
that love is interrupted by circumstances that there is
tension, which is resolved when the lovers are once
again in passionate embrace. It is a most simple and
basic view of life, not complicated with guilt, shame,
inhibition, or cultural expectations.

One might think that this worldview is reserved
for newly wedded teenagers who are deeply in love
and have no concept of the trials and difficulties life
can bring. But the author is mature, and he offers his
story as a norm. Herein is a philosophy of purity that
most people will never fathom. The very concept is
preposterous. Can erotic pleasure be as sacred as
prayer? Can the sensual and the spiritual both be the
creation of God, with equal standing?

Taking it further, could it be that God never
intended that tension should exist between flesh and
spirit? Surely he did not create opposing realities to
exist in conflict, but in balance, like positive and
negative charges. The atom with its opposite charges
is awhirl with energy, perfectly balanced, the building
block of all things. Without opposites and a balance of
tensions, there would be no energy, no motion. God
didn't intend for it to come down to one or the
other—flesh or spirit. Since the fall, we humans are
well aware of the contrariness of flesh and spirit. Only
in regeneration can we rediscover the harmony and
balance where "all things are pure."

The couple motivated by pure love ascends to true
humanity. Contrary to popular sentiment, it is only the
righteous who truly enjoy the pleasures of sexual

love. With the innocent and pure there is no imbalance, just the fullness that God intended when he conceived of his plan to place a naked couple in a beautiful garden of fruit and vegetables, flowers and herbs, spring water, and soft grass. The flesh and the spirit were to live in harmony as were the finite and the infinite. God created the flesh to give tangible expression to the spirit, and the spirit to raise the flesh above the animal and the temporal. The two dimensions of flesh and spirit, coupled with the third dimension of God, produced divine reality. Flesh and spirit in fellowship with God was paradise.

Paradise was lost originally when flesh took the lead without regard to the spirit. The finite left the infinite and felt its nakedness. The God of flesh and spirit postponed paradise. In time, God himself would be made sinless flesh and, in him, flesh would submit to spirit. There would be wholeness once again. But in the meantime, the Song of Solomon reminds us that married couples can still take excursions into paradise.

If you have lived a life of imbalance—all flesh, selfishly pursued, without godly love, if you have reason to be guilty, God still offers forgiveness to those who repent. If you are a righteous believer who has never "been to paradise," and for reasons unknown, your sex life is conducted in the dark chambers of guilt, and the flesh seems dirty, and your spirit is weighed down with shame, then please know that the Holy Spirit of God has lovingly and graciously inspired a book to purify your thinking.

The Script

The script requires five singing parts:

- Wife
- Husband
- Daughters of Jerusalem (an ensemble)
- The bride's father
- Siblings of the bride (a mixed trio or quartet)

In addition to the singers, there is a cast of shepherds, city guards, and soldiers to guard Solomon's bedroom.

As I prepared this work, I examined other commentaries to see whom they supposed was the speaker of each part of the book. Is the woman speaking of her man, or is he speaking of her? Is the woman speaking, or is it the daughters of Jerusalem? There was no absolute consensus. I must confess that in two or three places, it took me several weeks of vacillation before establishing my opinions. I am quite firm now as to the speaker in 98% of the text. If I am wrong in a few instances, it will not materially change the overall interpretation of the book.

According to the content of the song, I have divided the text into scenes, just as it may have been done when it was dramatized for public performance.

The Song of Songs, which is Solomon's

Scene 1
Chapter 1

1 The song of songs, which is Solomon's.

Woman to the daughters of Jerusalem:

2 Let him kiss me with the kisses of his mouth: *She is daydreaming of the possibilities.*

Woman to the man:

for thy love is better than wine.
3 Because of the savour of thy good ointments thy name is as ointment poured forth, therefore do the virgins love thee. *The virgins who attend weddings and support the bride, love him.*

4 Draw me, *[lead me forth—carry me along]* we *[she and the virgins—daughters of Jerusalem who attend her]* will run after thee: the king hath brought me into his chambers: *[as in bed chambers]* we will be glad and rejoice in thee, we *[she and all the virgins]* will remember thy love more than wine: the upright love thee.

Woman to the daughters of Jerusalem:

She recalls her thoughts concerning her former lack of confidence over her suntanned appearance.

5 I am black, but comely, *[She knows she is attractive in spite of the suntan]* **O ye daughters of Jerusalem, as the tents of Kedar** *[one of the twelve sons of Ishmael, a warlike nomadic people living in dark tents in the Eastern desert],* **as the curtains of Solomon.**

6 Look not upon me, because I am black, because the sun hath looked upon me: my mother's children *[apparently she had step-siblings]* **were angry with me;** *[mistreated by her step-brothers and sisters.]* **they made me the keeper of the vineyards** *[an outdoor job, exposed to the sun and elements, which gave her the dark complexion]***; but mine own vineyard** *[When she calls her body a vineyard, she directs us to the coming analogy—she is a vineyard of fruit to be eaten (8:12).]* **have I not kept.** *As a working girl, she had not given attention to her physical looks. In any culture except Hollywood, regardless of how dark or light-skinned one may be, the outdoor suntanned look is considered undesirable.*

Woman to the man:

7 Tell me, O thou whom my soul loveth *[deeper than just physical love],* **where thou feedest** *[feeds his flock of sheep],* **where thou makest thy flock to rest at noon:** *[She will seek him where he keeps his sheep. She would find him at noon so she can share his noon meal.]* **for why should I be as one that turneth aside by the flocks of thy companions?** *She asks for directions so that she would not end up* *entangling her flock with the flocks of other male shepherds.*

Man to woman:

8 If thou know not, *[where his flock is]* **O thou fairest among women, go thy way forth by the footsteps of the flock** *[follow the trail of the sheep]*, **and feed thy kids** *[She watched over young sheep as well.]* **beside the shepherds' tents.** *She is to seek protection by remaining close to the tents. He gives her common-sense directions, watching out for her welfare and providing for her to come into his workplace unmolested.*

9 I have compared thee, O my love, to a company of horses in Pharaoh's chariots. *[Well-bred, muscular, showy, exciting]*

Ladies, you may not feel that you could be compared to a company of horses in Pharaoh's army, sleek, muscular, showy, full of vitality, but when your husband is sexually aroused, his eyes lie to him, and he sees and feels just as did Solomon.

10 Thy cheeks are comely with rows of jewels, thy neck with chains of gold. *She wears jewelry to enhance her sensuality. Jewelry is feminine by its very nature and tends to emphasize the feminine delicateness.*

Daughters of Jerusalem:

11 We will make thee borders of gold with studs of silver. *When he showed attention to how she looked in jewels (verse 10), the virgins offered to assist her in preparing her garments for her man.*

Woman to daughters:

12 **While the king sitteth at his table, my spikenard sendeth forth the smell thereof.** *Spikenard was sometimes used on the hair. She allures him with her fragrant herbal oils.*

13 **A bundle of myrrh is my wellbeloved unto me** *[She associates his odor with the aromatic oil]*; **he shall lie all night betwixt my breasts.** *She desires to lie naked with him as close as possible.*

14 **My beloved is unto me as a cluster of camphire** *[flowers]* **in the vineyards of Engedi** *[a refreshing and beautiful spring in the desert].*

Man to the woman:

15 **Behold, thou art fair, my love; behold, thou art fair; thou hast doves' eyes.**

16 **Behold, thou art fair, my beloved, yea, pleasant: also our bed is green.** *This Hebrew word for "green" is more than just the color; it is used in reference to greenery—living plants, something flourishing, fresh, like the grass under a tree.*

17 **The beams of our house are cedar, and our rafters of fir.** *Since the bed is living greenery, we can assume that the rafters are tree branches. He appeals to her by describing the place where they will make love. It is outdoors, on the grass, under the trees. She likes the idea, for in the next verse she takes up his analogy.*

Chapter 2

Woman to the man:

1 **I am the rose of Sharon, and the lily of the**

valleys. *The Sharon valley was a common place to graze sheep—profuse with flowers in the spring. Based on his suggestions in 1:16-17 that their bed would be in the grass under the trees, she identifies herself with the rose and the lily growing on the ground.*

Man to the woman:

2 As the lily among thorns, so is my love *[his bride]* **among the daughters** *[daughters of Jerusalem]. He concurs with her analogy. The Sharon valley was arrayed with thorns. In comparison to her, all other women are thorns. The rose and the lily, which he called her in verse 1, are all the more lovely when growing among the thorns, as in the Sharon valley.*

Woman to daughters of Jerusalem:

3 As the apple tree among the trees of the wood, so is my beloved among the sons *[She returns his analogy given in the above verse. They will make love on the grass, under the trees. She is the lily growing on the ground, and he is the tree under which the lily grows.].* **I sat down under his shadow with great delight, and his fruit was sweet to my taste.** *[He was as an apple tree, and she was under him eating his fruit.]*

4 He brought me to the banqueting house *[She is calling their outdoor retreat a "banqueting house"],* **and his banner** *[a standard of identification]* **over me was love** *[In place of the banners that would be over them in a genuine banqueting house, as she looked up, she saw him looming over her, with the* *"rafters" of trees beyond.]*.

5 Stay *[keep me there]* **me with flagons** *[containers of wine]*, **comfort me with apples**: *[Her lovesickness (aroused condition) would be satisfied by drinking and eating of her man. See verses 1,3]* **for I am sick of love** *[lovesick to the point of weakness—sexually aroused to distraction]*.

6 His left hand is under my head, and his right hand doth embrace me *[After copulation he is asleep, as seen by the next verse.]*.

7 I charge you, O ye daughters of Jerusalem, by the roes, and by the hinds of the field, that ye stir not up, nor awake my love, till he please. *She would cuddle him to her breasts undisturbed until he is through sleeping.*

Scene 2

This is a drama of their separation.

Woman to daughters of Jerusalem:

This is a new section. Having culminated their lovemaking in 2:5, the story turns to a drama of his seeking to draw her into another outdoor experience of making love. He is far away in the hills of Lebanon, keeping his sheep; it is spring again, and she dreams of him.

8 The voice of my beloved! behold, he cometh leaping upon the mountains, skipping upon the hills. *That is the way a man comes home to a willing wife.*

9 My beloved is like a roe or a young hart: behold, he standeth behind our wall, he looketh forth at

the windows, shewing himself through the lattice. *He is there to call her out to join him in an outdoor experience of making love.*

10 My beloved spake, and said unto me,

Man to woman:

**Rise up, my love, my fair one, and come away.
11 For, lo, the winter is past, the rain is over and gone;
12 The flowers appear on the earth; the time of the singing of birds is come, and the voice of the turtle dove is heard in our land;
13 The fig tree putteth forth her green figs, and the vines with the tender grape give a good smell.** *[This recognizes the association of odors to the sex drive.]* **Arise, my love, my fair one, and come away.** *He desires to have her share the wonder of spring with all of its accompanying odors and sights. The sensual aspect of nature stirs a man and woman to companionship. He does not go with her; she goes with him.*
14 O my dove *[woman is the dove]*, **that art in the clefts of the rock, in the secret places of the stairs** *[a steep, winding, path outdoors. He is imagining her in the landscape about him]* **let me see thy countenance** *[she has a pleasant countenance]*, **let me hear thy voice; for sweet is thy voice, and thy countenance is comely.**

15 Take *[as in, take hold—capture, seize]* **us the foxes, the little foxes, that spoil the vines: for our vines have tender grapes.** *Since she is compared to a vineyard, the vines would represent them. Foxes eat* *grapes. Big foxes are easily kept out by good fencing, but little foxes, which seem less significant, can slip through the small places. Likewise, it is the little things in a marriage that can spoil the delicate and tender relationship. So he covenants with her to be on guard against all such things.*

Woman to the man:

16 My beloved is mine, and I am his: he feedeth *[This word is used for feeding sheep.]* **among the lilies.** *She is as lilies (2:1). His "feeding" is metaphoric of her body, for sheep do not feed at night (verse 17).*

17 Until the day break, and the shadows flee away, turn *[to come back]*, **my beloved, and be thou like a roe or a young hart upon the mountains of Bether.** *Come to her quickly.*

Chapter 3
Woman to daughters of Jerusalem:

1 By night on my bed I sought him whom my soul loveth: I sought him, but I found him not.
2 I will rise now, and go about the city in the streets, and in the broad ways I will seek him whom my soul loveth: I sought him, but I found him not.
3 The watchmen that go about the city found me: to whom I said, Saw ye him whom my soul loveth?
4 It was but a little that I passed from them, but I found him whom my soul loveth: I held him, and would not let him go *[persistent]*, **until I had brought him into my mother's house, and into the**

chamber of her that conceived me. *She was aggressive and not abashed to take the lead in lovemaking.*

5 I charge you, O ye daughters of Jerusalem, by the roes, and by the hinds of the field, that ye stir not up, nor awake my love, till he please. *She awoke in the night with a passion to lie with her husband, so she went out and pursued him until she had him back home. He now sleeps the rest of the night.*

Scene 3

Up until now, the couple could have been any pair of lowly shepherds, but the song at this point takes on a royal perspective.

Daughters of Jerusalem to each other:

6 Who is this that cometh out of the wilderness like pillars of smoke, perfumed with myrrh and frankincense, with all powders of the merchant? *He comes home with a rush, exuding power. He has anointed himself with natural odors of the wilderness so as to appeal to her sexual drives. Their goal is the bed—next verse.*

7 Behold his bed, which is Solomon's; threescore valiant men are about it, of the valiant of Israel. 8 They all hold swords, being expert in war: every man hath his sword upon his thigh because of fear in the night. *The women exulted in his physical prowess.*

9 King Solomon made himself a chariot of the

wood of Lebanon.

10 He made the pillars thereof of silver, the bottom thereof of gold, the covering of it of purple, the midst thereof being paved with love, for the daughters of Jerusalem. *They brag on his power and the beauty of the bed on which he makes love and the chariot in which he rides.*

Bride to daughters of Jerusalem:

11 Go forth, O ye daughters of Zion, and behold king Solomon with the crown wherewith his mother crowned him in the day of his espousals *[Apparently his mother, Bathsheba, placed the crown on his head on the same day that he was espoused to the woman of this song.],* **and in the day of the gladness of his heart.** *She reminds them of her husband's position and sends them out to greet him in his majestic return. She takes pride in him and brags to the other women.*

Chapter 4

Man to the woman:

1 Behold, thou art fair, my love; behold, thou art fair; thou hast doves' eyes within thy locks *[Her hair is around her face and frames her eyes.]:* **thy hair is as a flock of goats, that appear from mount Gilead.** *A flock of goats coming down the mountain spill forth as a long widening line, like a woman's long hair spilling over her shoulders.*

2 Thy teeth are like a flock of sheep that are even shorn *[same length],* **which came up from the washing** *[very white];* **whereof every one bear**

twins, and none is barren among them *[no missing teeth]*.
3 Thy lips are like a thread of scarlet, and thy speech is comely *[Her words are profitable and wholesome]*: **thy temples are like a piece of a pomegranate** *[blushed]* **within thy locks.**
4 Thy neck is like the tower of David builded for an armoury, *[strong and polished]* **whereon there hang a thousand bucklers, all shields of mighty men.** *[feeling of power in her neck]*
5 Thy two breasts are like two young roes that are twins, which feed among the lilies *[serene, noble, wholesome—pulsating with each breath]*.
6 Until the day break, and the shadows flee away, I will get me to the mountain of myrrh, and to the hill of frankincense *[speaks of love in the night hours. She is as myrrh to him (4:14; 5:1, 4). She is frankincense (4:14)]*.

7 Thou art all fair, my love; there is no spot in thee *[no moral blemish]*.
8 Come with me from Lebanon, my spouse, with me from Lebanon: look from the top of Amana, from the top of Shenir and Hermon *[mountains in Lebanon]*, **from the lions' dens** *[high and inaccessible]*, **from the mountains of the leopards.** *He invites her to join him in the mountains, in lofty, serene places. He would share the beauty of the high country. Men tend to associate the beauty and stillness of nature with the romantic. A man wants to share his appreciation of nature with his wife. What better way than to bring her into the place he so loves?*

9 Thou hast ravished my heart, my sister, *[she arouses him to distraction]* **my spouse;** *[she is his wife]* **thou hast ravished my heart with one of thine eyes** *[a woman's eyes have great seductive powers]*, **with one chain of thy neck.** *Jewelry projects femininity and sexuality.*
10 How fair is thy love, my sister, my spouse! *[She is his wife]* **how much better is thy love than wine!** *[Instead of driving him to drink, she drives him to herself.]* **and the smell of thine ointments than all spices!** *He associates her scent with culinary spices.*
11 Thy lips, O my spouse, drop as the honeycomb: *[When a woman is aroused, her lips turn fiery pink and moist, enticing the man. Thus, women paint their lips and redden their cheeks to appear sexually aroused.]* **honey and milk are under thy tongue** *[They practice deep kissing]*; **and the smell of thy garments is like the smell of Lebanon.** *Her smell reminds him of the cleanness of the outdoors.*

12 A garden inclosed is my sister, my spouse; a spring shut up, a fountain sealed. *He compares her to a private garden, filled with flowers and fruit, with a pure spring, enclosed and uncontaminated as a virgin.*
13 Thy plants *[She is a garden, thus she has plants— her body parts.]* **are an orchard of pomegranates, with pleasant fruits; camphire, with spikenard,**
14 Spikenard and saffron; calamus and cinnamon, with all trees of frankincense; myrrh and aloes, with all the chief spices: *Research has shown that cinnamon and other culinary spices excite a man's sexual senses, whereas artificial perfumes diminish a*

man's drive. All of the above spices and fruits come from the 'garden' of her body.
15 A fountain of gardens, a well of living waters, and streams from Lebanon. *She is not stagnant water, but living water, flowing, alive, bubbly, and refreshing.*

Woman to man:

16 Awake, O north wind; and come, thou south; blow upon my garden *[He just said she was a garden in verse 12]*, **that the spices thereof may flow out.** *[She promises that her body will flow with juices in preparation for her man.]* **Let my beloved come into his garden, and eat his pleasant fruits.** *The garden is her body, and the pleasant fruits are the erotic pleasures she offers.*

Chapter 5
Man to woman:

1 I am come into my garden, my sister, my spouse: I have gathered my myrrh with my spice *(4:13)*; **I have eaten my honeycomb** *[her lips, (4:11]* **with my honey** *[honey and milk are under her tongue, 4:11]*; **I have drunk my wine with my milk:** *(4:11).* *They have shared foreplay and copulated.*

Man to general audience

eat, O friends; drink, yea, drink abundantly, *[Drink of the body of your spouse, for she is a spring, a fountain (4:12.)]* **O beloved.** *He turns to the audience and exhorts them to have abundant erotic pleasures as he has done.*

Scene 4

The following is a crisis in the drama of their lovemaking.

Woman tells her experience to the audience:

2 I sleep, but my heart waketh: it is the voice of my beloved that knocketh, saying, *[In a half-wakened state, she hears him knocking.]*

Man said to woman:

Open to me, my sister, my love, my dove, my undefiled: for my head is filled with dew, and my locks with the drops of the night. *He has come to her in the night and is wet with dew.*

Woman speaks to her man:

3 I have put off my coat; how shall I put it on? I have washed my feet; how shall I defile them? *She did not want to be inconvenienced, so she tells him that it is not a good time.*

Woman narrates to daughters of Jerusalem:

4 My beloved put in his hand by the hole of the door, *[He tried to untie the door]* **and my bowels were moved for him.** *She was sexually aroused when he was persistent to get to her.*
5 I rose up to open to my beloved; and my hands dropped with myrrh, and my fingers with sweet smelling myrrh, upon the handles of the lock. *She is now ready for him. Her juices are flowing.*

6 I opened to my beloved; but my beloved had withdrawn himself, *[She responded too slowly, and he departed.]* **and was gone: my soul failed when he spake** *[she recalls]*: **I sought him, but I could not find him; I called him, but he gave me no answer.** *She waited until she was aroused before she inconvenienced herself. If she had responded to his need, the following tragedy would not have occurred.*

7 The watchmen that went about the city found me, they smote me, they wounded me; the keepers of the walls took away my veil from me. *When she refused him, she got out from under his headship, which took her into places where she was subject to attack.*

8 I charge you, O daughters of Jerusalem, if ye find my beloved, that ye tell him, that I am sick of love. *She is highly aroused.*

Daughters of Jerusalem ask woman:

9 What is thy beloved more than another beloved, O thou fairest among women? what is thy beloved more than another beloved, that thou dost so charge us? *The daughters of Jerusalem pose a rhetorical question designed to give her the opportunity to extol her beloved: "Why is this man so special?"*

Woman answers daughters of Jerusalem by describing his physical characteristics:

10 My beloved is white and ruddy *[red],* **the chiefest among ten thousand.** *She is confident that he is the pick among 10,000 men.*

11 His head is as the most fine gold, his locks are bushy, and black as a raven. *[thick, slightly curly, black hair]*

12 His eyes are as the eyes of doves by the rivers of waters, washed with milk, and fitly set.

13 His cheeks are as a bed of spices, as sweet flowers: his lips like lilies, dropping sweet smelling myrrh. *She is drawn to his lips. The text reveals the analogy between the body and various tasty fruits and aromatic spices.*

14 His hands are as gold rings set with the beryl *[a precious stone, sea green]*: **his belly is as bright ivory overlaid with sapphires.** *She is attracted to his belly and admires the transparent blue stones that overlay it. Leviticus 21:20 and Deuteronomy 23:1 refer to a man's testicles as "stones."*

15 His legs are as pillars of marble, set upon sockets of fine gold *[She admires the strength and beauty of his legs]*: **his countenance is as Lebanon, excellent as the cedars.** *It is his body that most captivates her, but she appreciates his countenance also.*

16 His mouth is most sweet *[Again she is attracted to his mouth]*: **yea, he is altogether lovely.** *[Her answer reveals her preoccupation with his body. It is as though she is worshipping him.]* **This is my beloved, and this is my friend** *[He is more than her lover. He has become her friend.]*, **O daughters of Jerusalem.** *She never speaks disparagingly of her husband to other women.*

Chapter 6
Daughters of Jerusalem ask woman:

They must have been satisfied with her answer as to why he was so special, for they are now prepared to help her search.

1 Whither is thy beloved gone, O thou fairest among women? whither is thy beloved turned aside? that we may seek him with thee.

Woman answers daughters:

2 My beloved is gone down into his garden *(She is the garden 4:12)*, **to the beds of spices** *(She is the spices 4:13-14, 16)*, **to feed in the gardens, and to gather lilies.**
3 I am my beloved's, and my beloved is mine: he feedeth among the lilies. *She is the lilies (2:1). This is metaphoric of foreplay.*

Man to woman:

4 Thou art beautiful, O my love, as Tirzah *[A beautiful city that once rivaled Jerusalem as the capital]*, **comely as Jerusalem, terrible as an army with banners.**
5 Turn away thine eyes from me, for they have overcome me *[A woman's eyes have great seductive powers]*: **thy hair is as a flock of goats that appear from Gilead.**
6 Thy teeth are as a flock of sheep which go up from the washing, whereof every one beareth twins, and there is not one barren among them.
7 As a piece of a pomegranate are thy temples

within thy locks. *[Her hair is not pulled back away from her temples.]*

Man to audience:

8 There are threescore queens, and fourscore concubines, and virgins without number.
9 My dove, my undefiled is but one; she is the only one of her mother, *[indicating that her sisters were not from her mother]* **she is the choice one of her that bare her. The daughters saw her, and blessed her; yea, the queens and the concubines, and they praised her.** *She earned their praise.*

Daughters of Jerusalem:

This is a follow-up of the former statement that the daughters blessed her and praised her.

10 Who is she that looketh forth as the morning *[Fresh, clean, bright-eyed]*, **fair as the moon, clear as the sun** *[open and transparent]*, **and <u>terrible</u> as an army with banners?** *She has presence.*

Woman to daughters:

She had been looking for him, but has made a trip to the garden, when he returns.

11 I went down into the garden of nuts to see the fruits of the valley, and to see whether the vine flourished, and the pomegranates budded. *It is she who goes to the garden, for in verse 13, the daughters of Jerusalem appeal to her to return.*
12 Or ever I was aware *[Before she was made aware that he was looking for her—inviting her to join him*

on an outing 7:11], **my soul made me like the chariots of Amminadib.** *[to come swiftly before she even heard that he was looking for her] She was motivated by intuition to hasten her return. Women come to have extra-sensory awareness concerning their husbands.*

Daughters of Jerusalem to the woman:

13 Return, return, O Shulamite *[She is called by the name of the insignificant town from which she came, as if to draw attention to the great advances she has made in being sought by the king.];* **return, return, that we may look upon thee.** *They would see her again through his eyes.*

Daughters of Jerusalem to the man:

What will ye see in the Shulamite? As it were the company of two armies. *He spoke of her as an army (6:10). After hearing his wonderful description of her, the daughters of Jerusalem want to view her again in light of his praise. A man's high public estimation of his wife will elevate her in the eyes of others.*

Chapter 7
Man to woman:

He is answering 6:13b as to what he sees in the Shulamite.

1 How beautiful are thy feet with shoes, O prince's daughter! the joints of thy thighs *[The Hebrew root for the word translated "thighs" means "to be soft," and refers to the outside portion of the hips where the* *legs meet the torso. We call that the hips.]* **are like jewels, the work of the hands of a cunning workman.** *He was attracted to her soft, well-formed hips.*

2 Thy navel is like a round goblet, which wanteth not liquor: thy belly *[the part below her navel]* **is like an heap of wheat** *[golden—good to eat]* **set about with lilies** *[pubic hair].*

The Hebrew word "beten," translated "belly" here, is found 72 times in the O. T., and it is translated belly 30 times, womb 31, body 8, within 2, and born 1.

3 Thy two breasts are like two young roes that are twins. *See 4:5.*

4 Thy neck is as a tower of ivory; thine eyes like the fishpools in Heshbon, by the gate of Bathrabbim: thy nose is as the tower of Lebanon which looketh toward Damascus. *Apparently he considered a distinctive, strong nose to be quite attractive.*

5 Thine head upon thee is like Carmel *[a towering mountain above the sea of Galilee],* **and the hair of thine head like purple; the king is held in the galleries** *[He is captivated to look upon her].*

6 How fair and how pleasant art thou, O love, for delights!

7 This thy stature is like to a palm tree, and thy breasts to clusters of grapes.

8 I said, I will go up to the palm tree *[her torso],* **I will take hold of the boughs thereof** *[her limbs]:* **now also thy breasts shall be as clusters of the vine** *[he would eat her breasts as one eats grapes],* **and the smell of thy nose like apples;**

9 And the roof of thy mouth *[deep kissing]* **like the**

best wine for my beloved, that goeth down sweetly, causing the lips of those that are asleep to speak. *She is intoxicating, causing him to talk in his sleep.*

Woman to daughters:

She responds to the above answer that he gave as to why she is so special.

10 I am my beloved's, and his desire is toward me. *She revels in his passion for her body and employs it to attract him.*

Woman to man:

11 Come, my beloved, let us go forth into the field *[translated field, country, and wild]*; **let us lodge in the villages.** *She desires to take a romantic excursion with him into the country.*

12 Let us get up early to the vineyards *[She has defined herself as a vineyard, as has he. 1:6; 7:7]*; **let us see if the vine flourish, whether the tender grape appear** *[her breasts]*, **and the pomegranates bud forth** *[her temples blushed with passion]*: **there will I give thee my loves.** *They make love outdoors in the garden.*

13 The mandrakes *[used as an aphrodisiac]* **give a smell, and at our gates are all manner of pleasant fruits,** *[aspects of their bodies]* **new** *[also translated "new thing"]* **and old, which I have laid up for thee, O my beloved.** *She is prepared to engage in old techniques of foreplay and has also developed something new for him. She is making sure their love life does not get boring.*

Chapter 8

Woman to man:

1 O that thou wert as my brother, that sucked the breasts of my mother! when I should find thee without, I would kiss thee; yea, I should not be despised. *She desires that he be as near to her as her little brother was to his mother, always close, sucking her breasts. She is comfortable comparing their intimacy to the intimacy of an infant and his mother.* **2 I would lead thee, and bring thee into my mother's house, who would instruct me** *[Her mother would give her instruction on matters of sex]*: **I would cause thee to drink of spiced wine of the juice of my pomegranate** *[not just any pomegranate, but the metaphoric fruit of her body—4:12].*

Woman to the daughters of Jerusalem:

3 His left hand should be under my head, and his right hand should *[In 2:6 she said, "doth embrace," not "should embrace," as she does here. She is dreaming in his absence.]* **embrace me.** *[When he is asleep—see next verse.] This is not their foreplay position. Both times when this position is mentioned, he is asleep.* **4 I charge you, O daughters of Jerusalem, that ye stir not up, nor awake my love, until he please.** *It was her tenderness toward him after copulation that caused her to protectively embrace him and guard his privacy as he slept.*

Father of the Woman:

Her father sees them coming. When sung, this would

be a rousing, powerful refrain, sung with joy and celebration.

5 Who is this that cometh up from the wilderness, leaning upon her beloved? *[Her father sees her coming from the wilderness where they made love and slept the night.]* **I raised thee up under the apple tree: there thy mother brought thee forth: there she brought thee forth that bare thee.** *Father raised his daughter under the same apple tree under which she was born. This reveals her affinity for the apple tree and why it is so dear to her as to use it as an analogy for her husband.*

6 Set me as a seal upon thine heart, as a seal upon thine arm: *[Her father challenges her to accept his instruction—probably in matters of marital love—and metaphorically compares it to a seal of sacred scripture that the Jews placed on their arms, next to their hearts.]* **for love is strong as death; jealousy is cruel as the grave: the coals thereof are coals of fire, which hath a most vehement flame.** *He warns her to abide in love and to not allow the fires of jealousy to destroy her marriage.*

7 Many waters cannot quench love, neither can the floods drown it: *[Marital love is the most powerful and consuming force on the planet.]* **if a man would give all the substance of his house for love, it would utterly be contemned** *[despised]*. *Love cannot be purchased.*

Scene 5

Siblings, said of the woman when she was young:

After the success of their lovemaking, the song exults in her triumph over earlier criticism from her step-family. This is also a celebration.

8 We have a little sister, and she hath no breasts: what shall we do for our sister in the day when she shall be spoken for? *[They were either concerned, or they were making fun of her for developing late.]*
9 If she be a wall, we will build upon her a palace of silver *[If she remained flat-chested, they would compensate with silver decorations]*: **and if she be a door, we will inclose her with boards of cedar.** *A plain door can be made attractive with decorative casements.*

Woman to audience:

She brags of her eventual development—full breasts.

10 I am a wall, and my breasts like towers: then was I in his eyes as one that found favour. *She found favor because of her protruding breasts.*

11 Solomon had *["had"—past tense; she is telling a story from his past]* **a vineyard at Baalhamon; he let out the vineyard unto keepers; every one for the fruit thereof was to bring a thousand pieces of silver.** *She takes note of a fact concerning a valuable vineyard. Each worker was expected to produce a return of 1000 pieces of silver, given to Solomon.*

12 My vineyard, which is mine, is before me *[her*

body (1:6)]: **thou, O Solomon, must have a thousand, and those that keep the fruit thereof two hundred.** *The vineyard was to produce 1200 pieces of silver and the workers were to get one-sixth, 200, whereas the owner, Solomon, was to get 1000. She is offering him her metaphoric garden in contrast to his former vineyard that paid so well. Solomon was the keeper of her vineyard (her body), and so he should reap the benefit of it.*

Woman to the man:

13 Thou that dwellest in the gardens, the companions hearken to thy voice: cause me to hear it. *His companions in labor have the privilege of hearing his voice. She desires the same, offering him a better vineyard.*

14 Make haste, my beloved, and be thou like to a roe or to a young hart upon the mountains of spices. *She craves his swift return to the mountain of spices—her body.*

Examining Additional Scripture

In the beginning God created sex

God **"at the beginning made them male and female"** *(Genesis 2:35).* Think about it. It was God's idea to make his creation into sexual counterparts with all that is implied. He said that a man should **cleave** unto his wife, and merge into **one flesh.** When a couple comes together sexually, it is declared to be God **joining** them together *(Matthew 19:6).*

God delights to see people experience the fulfillment of marriage, so that **"Whoso findeth a wife findeth a good thing, and obtaineth favour of the LORD"** *(Proverbs 18:22).* If one obtains favor with God by getting married, then marriage is a higher state than celibacy. **"A prudent wife is from the LORD"** *(Proverbs 19:14).*

The sinful use made of the sex drive has not tainted the concept itself, for we read that marriage remains **"honourable in all, and the bed undefiled"** *(Hebrews 13:4).*

"There be three things which are too wonderful for me, yea, four which I know not: The way of an eagle in the air; the way of a serpent upon a rock; the way of a ship in the midst of the

sea; and the way of a man with a maid" *(Proverbs 30:18-19).* The fourth thing—*"the way of a man with a maid"*—was so wonderful to behold that it was beyond human comprehension.

God's bride

The Bible reveals God's attitude toward sex, in that when God wanted the nation of Israel to understand how he felt toward them, he chose marriage for his analogy. Speaking as the bridegroom, he said to the nation of Israel: **"I will even betroth thee unto me in faithfulness: and thou shalt know the LORD"** *(Hosea 2:20).* God's view of the sanctity of marital love led him to say to Israel, **"as the bridegroom rejoiceth over the bride, so shall thy God rejoice over thee"** *(Isaiah 62:5).*

Through the prophet Jeremiah, God reminded Israel of their earlier courtship when the nation loved him and pursued him as a bride seeks her husband: **"I remember thee, the kindness of thy youth, the love of thine espousals, when thou wentest after me in the wilderness...."** *(Jeremiah 2:2-3).*

The prophet Isaiah reminded Israel: **"<u>Thy Maker is thine husband</u>; the LORD of hosts is his name; and thy Redeemer the Holy One of Israel; The God of the whole earth shall he be called. For the LORD hath called thee as a woman forsaken and grieved in spirit, and a wife of youth, when thou wast refused, saith thy God"** *(Isaiah 54:5-7).*

When Israel went after strange gods, God called it adultery and commanded, **"Turn, O backsliding**

children, saith the LORD; <u>for I am married unto</u>
<u>you</u>: and I will take you one of a city, and two of a
family, and I will bring you to Zion" *(Jeremiah*
3:14).

Again Jeremiah quotes God as saying, "<u>I was an</u>
<u>husband</u> unto them, saith the LORD" *(Jeremiah*
31:32).

God takes a bride to his bed

When Israel turned away from her "husband" to
worship idols, God sent word to them through
Ezekiel, calling them to repentance. God compared
himself to a man finding a castoff infant girl and
raising her until she is old enough to become his wife.
In the analogy, the man, which typifies God, is
attracted to the mature body of the woman and takes
her to his bridal bed.

> *Ezekiel 16:1-14*
> **1 Again the word of the LORD came unto me,**
> **saying,**
> **2 Son of man, cause Jerusalem to know her**
> **abominations,**
> **3 And say, Thus saith the Lord GOD unto**
> **Jerusalem; Thy birth and thy nativity is of the**
> **land of Canaan; thy father was an Amorite,**
> **and thy mother an Hittite.** *[insulting]*
> **4 And as for thy nativity, in the day thou wast**
> **born thy navel was not cut, neither wast thou**
> **washed in water to supple thee; thou wast not**
> **salted at all, nor swaddled at all.**
> **5 None eye pitied thee, to do any of these unto**
> **thee, to have compassion upon thee; but thou**

wast cast out in the open field, to the lothing of
thy person, in the day that thou wast born.
6 And when I passed by thee, and saw thee
polluted in thine own blood, I said unto thee
when thou wast in thy blood, Live; yea, I said
unto thee when thou wast in thy blood, Live.
7 I have caused thee to multiply as the bud of
the field, and thou hast increased and waxen
great, and thou art come to excellent
ornaments: <u>thy breasts are fashioned, and thine
hair is grown, whereas thou wast naked and
bare</u>.
8 Now when I passed by thee, and looked upon
thee, behold, <u>thy time was the time of love; and
I spread my skirt over thee, and covered thy
nakedness</u>: yea, I sware unto thee, and entered
into a covenant with thee, saith the Lord GOD,
<u>and thou becamest mine</u>.
9 Then washed I thee with water; <u>yea, I
throughly washed away thy blood from thee,
and I anointed thee with oil</u>.
10 I clothed thee also with broidered work, and
shod thee with badgers' skin, and I girded thee
about with fine linen, and I covered thee with
silk.
11 I decked thee also with ornaments, and I put
bracelets upon thy hands, and a chain on thy
neck.
12 And I put a jewel on thy forehead, and
earrings in thine ears, and a beautiful crown
upon thine head.
13 Thus wast thou decked with gold and silver;
and thy raiment was of fine linen, and silk, and

broidered work; thou didst eat fine flour, and honey, and oil: and thou wast exceeding beautiful, and thou didst prosper into a kingdom.

14 And thy renown went forth among the heathen for thy beauty: for it was perfect through my comeliness, which I had put upon thee, saith the Lord GOD.

In verse 8, God, speaking of himself as a man desiring a woman, said, **"thy time was the time of love; and I spread my skirt over thee, and covered thy nakedness."** This is a description of a man mating with his new bride. She had been a virgin, for God said that following copulation, he washed away her blood and anointed her with oil (verse 9). By employing this graphic analogy, God is reminding Israel of her disreputable beginning and of the holiness and purity to which he has brought her as a nation.

If it seems totally inappropriate to you for God to depict himself as a husband copulating with his wife, "you do err, not knowing the scriptures!" If you feel that erotic pleasure between a man and his wife is beneath the holiness of God, that it is not as high and holy as is purest worship, you are out of sync with God, and your conscience needs divine instruction. Don't stop reading now.

Jesus the bridegroom

The entire forty-fifth Psalm is dedicated to comparing the love of Christ and the church to the love of a man and a woman. This inspired text calls it **"A Song of**

loves." It represents the love of Christ to his church in images that are similar to those in the Song of Solomon. Verses 6 and 7 are quoted in Hebrews 1:8-9 as a prophecy of Messiah. In verse 11, the bride is told that the groom is her **Lord** and that she should **worship him**—just what you would expect of deity, not David. Verse 2 says that the groom of this song is **fairer than the children of men,** indicating that he is more than a mere man. And verse 17 says, **"the people shall praise thee for ever and ever."** In verses 7 and 8 God speaks to God. That is, God the Father speaks to God the Son concerning the anointing he will receive.

Psalm 45
A Song of loves.
1 My heart is inditing a good matter: I speak of the things which I have made touching the king: my tongue is the pen of a ready writer.
2 Thou art fairer than the children of men: grace is poured into thy lips: therefore God hath blessed thee for ever.
3 Gird thy sword upon thy thigh, O most mighty, with thy glory and thy majesty.
6 Thy throne, O God, is for ever and ever: the sceptre of thy kingdom is a right sceptre.
7 Thou lovest righteousness, and hatest wickedness: therefore God, thy God, hath anointed thee with the oil of gladness above thy fellows. *[Verses 6-7 are quoted in Hebrews 1:8-9.]*
8 All thy garments smell of myrrh, and aloes, and cassia, out of the ivory palaces, whereby they have made thee glad.

9 Kings' daughters were among thy honourable women: upon thy right hand did stand the queen in gold of Ophir.
10 Hearken, O daughter, and consider, and incline thine ear; forget also thine own people, and thy father's house;
11 So shall the king greatly desire thy beauty: for he is thy Lord; and worship thou him.
12 And the daughter of Tyre shall be there with a gift; even the rich among the people shall intreat thy favour.
13 The king's daughter is all glorious within: her clothing is of wrought gold.
14 She shall be brought unto the king in raiment of needlework: the virgins her companions that follow her shall be brought unto thee.
15 With gladness and rejoicing shall they be brought: they shall enter into the king's palace.
16 Instead of thy fathers shall be thy children, whom thou mayest make princes in all the earth.
17 I will make thy name to be remembered in all generations: therefore shall the people praise thee for ever and ever.

Marriage Analogy

In the New Testament, we find the marriage analogy used frequently. **"The kingdom of heaven is like unto a certain king, which made a marriage for his son"** *(Matthew 22:2).*

- John the Baptist called Jesus the bridegroom and

referred to himself as the friend of the bridegroom (the best man at the wedding). **"He that hath the bride** *[the church]* **is the bridegroom** *[Jesus]***: but the friend of the bridegroom** *[John]***, which standeth and heareth him, rejoiceth greatly because of the bridegroom's voice** *[the voice of Jesus]***: this my joy therefore is fulfilled"** *(John 3:29)*.

• The apostle Paul said that his ministry was to prepare the bride of Christ (in this case the church at Corinth) for the bridegroom: **"For I have espoused you to one husband, that I may present you as a chaste virgin to Christ"** *(2 Corinthians 11:2)*.

• Jesus also employed the analogy of marriage to himself. **"And Jesus said unto them, Can the children of the bridechamber mourn, as long as the bridegroom is with them? but the days will come, when the bridegroom shall be taken from them, and then shall they fast"** *(Matthew 9:15)*.

• In the book of Ephesians, Paul says that a husband should love his wife— the woman with whom he is one flesh—as Christ loves the church, with whom he is one flesh. Then he tells us that the one-flesh union of a man and his wife and of Christ and his church is a mystery.

Ephesians 5:28-32
28 So ought men to love their wives as their own bodies. He that loveth his wife loveth himself.
29 For no man ever yet hated his own flesh; but nourisheth and cherisheth it, even as the Lord the church:

30 For we are members of his body, of his flesh, and of his bones. *Just as a man and his wife are one flesh, so the church is Christ's bride and one flesh with him.*
31 For this cause shall a man leave his father and mother, and shall be joined unto his wife, and they two shall be one flesh.
32 This is a great mystery: but I speak concerning Christ and the church. *The closest analogy to Christ and the church is the one flesh sexual union that occurs in marriage.*

• In the last book of the Bible, the apostle John is transported into the future and sees the marriage of Christ to his church. The church is called **his wife**.

Revelation 19:7-9
7 Let us be glad and rejoice, and give honour to him: for the marriage of the Lamb is come, and <u>his wife</u> hath made herself ready.
8 And to her was granted that she should be arrayed in fine linen, clean and white: for the fine linen is the righteousness of saints.
9 And he saith unto me, Write, Blessed are they which are called unto the marriage supper of the Lamb. And he saith unto me, These are the true sayings of God."

• Paul tells the believers that salvation is embodied in what he calls a marriage to Jesus Christ. **"Ye also are become dead to the law by the body of Christ; that <u>ye should be married to another</u>, even to him who is raised from the dead, that we should bring forth fruit unto God"** *(Romans 7:4).*

• At the end of the final age **"John saw the holy**

city, new Jerusalem, coming down from God out of heaven, prepared as a bride adorned for her husband" *(Revelation 21:2).*

•   After this present world has been destroyed and eternity has begun, the angel says to John concerning the church, **"Come hither, I will shew thee the bride, the Lamb's wife"** *(Revelation 21:9).* So in eternity the church will relate to God as a bride to her husband.

•   And in the very last chapter of Revelation, in verse 17, the Holy Spirit joins with the Bride, inviting others to come up to be with them for eternity.

In the first moments of eternity, when the bridegroom takes the church home to his house, when the honeymoon begins, the consummation of the marriage will be a spiritual orgasm of joy which the fleshly analogy could only dimly foreshadow.

Regeneration likened to reproduction

The Bible everywhere depicts regeneration as being "born again." For one to be born, there must first be a conception. Conception is the coming together of two realities—the sperm and the egg—from which a new life is conceived and begins to grow towards birth. Peter said it plainly, **"Being born again, not of <u>corruptible seed</u>, but of incorruptible, by the word of God, which liveth and abideth for ever"** *(1 Peter 1:23).* Natural birth takes place when **corruptible seed** *(male sperm)* fertilizes the female egg. The new birth takes place when the **incorruptible seed** *(the* *word of God)* fertilizes the human spirit.

The process of producing children is called *begetting*. The word *begat*, in several forms, is used 227 times in the Bible in phrases like, **"And he begat many sons and daughters."** James says of the new birth, **"Of his own will <u>begat he us</u> with the word of truth..."** *(James 1:18).* Peter speaks in like manner: **"Blessed be the God and Father of our Lord Jesus Christ, which according to his abundant mercy hath <u>begotten us</u> again unto a lively hope by the resurrection of Jesus Christ from the dead"** *(1 Peter 1:3-5).*

John carries the idea further with the allusion to natural conception when he says, **"Whosoever is born of God doth not commit sin; for <u>his seed remaineth in him</u>: and he cannot sin, because he is born of God"** *(1 John 3:9).* The believer has the power to overcome sin because the **seed**—just like the sperm that generated life—which is the Word of God, remains in him. He is a new creature, having been reborn of a Heavenly Father.

Since God compares the words of Holy Scripture to male sperm, it must be that the human reproductive process is created in the image of divine realities.

John 3:3-7
**3 Jesus answered and said unto him, Verily, verily, I say unto thee, Except a man be born again, he cannot see the kingdom of God.
4 Nicodemus saith unto him, How can a man be born when he is old? can he enter the second time into his mother's womb, and be born?**

5 Jesus answered, Verily, verily, I say unto thee, Except a man be born of water (natural birth) and of the Spirit, he cannot enter into the kingdom of God.
6 That which is born of the flesh is flesh; and that which is born of the Spirit is spirit.
7 Marvel not that I said unto thee, Ye must be born again.

Two births—one by water and one by spirit. Flesh gives birth to flesh, and Spirit gives birth to spirit. As the natural birth is delivered by water in the womb, the spiritual birth is delivered by the Spirit. This has nothing to do with water baptism. Natural birth is a watery affair.

The newly born-again person is a **"newborn babe"** and is told to **"desire the sincere milk of the word, that ye may grow thereby"** *(1 Peter 2:2).*

The Bible says in 1 Corinthians 6:15-17, of those who have been born again, that their **"bodies are the members of Christ?"** and that the one who is **"joined unto the Lord is one spirit."** This oneness with Christ's body maintains the parallel of fleshly union.

When the church at Galatia began to fall away from Christ, Paul employed the birth analogy to define his intentions: **"My little children, of whom I travail in birth again until Christ be formed in you"** *(Galatians 4:19).*

Virgin conception

God used conception and childbirth to bring Jesus into

the world. The Bible speaks of a **mystery**—something clouded in the strange and secret. Paul said that no one would debate the greatness of this mystery. **"And without controversy great is the mystery of godliness: God was manifest in the flesh, justified in the Spirit, seen of angels, preached unto the Gentiles, believed on in the world, received up into glory"** *(1 Timothy 3:16)*. God, the eternal spirit, the first cause, the prime mover, became flesh!

Has the ecclesiastical ritualization of this event desensitized you to its wonder? Let me say it another way: God became a fetus. Or, to be more clinical, God became 23 human chromosomes in a single sperm created by God to fertilize the egg of a virgin who also carried 23 human chromosomes. The sperm of God fertilized the egg of the woman and the chromosomes combined to make 46, the first cell of a living soul who was both God and human. Infinite God and finite man merged to become one person in the womb of a virgin. A wonderful mystery indeed!

The great miracle was not that a virgin gave birth, but that a virgin conceived through Divine insemination. The angel said to the virgin, **"Thou shalt <u>conceive in thy womb</u>, and bring forth a son, and shalt call his name JESUS"** *(Luke 1:31)*. Most people have never dared reflect on the fact that the Bible calls it a *conception.* It is easier to think that somehow God placed a perfect baby in the womb of the virgin, or that he took possession of the soul of a human baby—neither of which is true. Conception is a natural human process of the sperm entering the egg and fertilizing it. The angel told Joseph, **"that which** is <u>conceived</u> in her is of the Holy Ghost" *(Matthew 1:20).*

We must keep in mind that Jesus was human as well as God. The process of conception was completely natural with the exception that she was not penetrated. She felt nothing. When the angel told Mary of God's intentions, Mary said to the angel, **"How shall this be, seeing I know not a man? And the angel answered and said unto her, The Holy Ghost shall come upon thee, and the <u>power of the Highest shall overshadow thee</u>: therefore also that holy thing which shall be born of thee shall be called the Son of God"** *(Luke 1:34-35).* The Holy Spirit of God overshadowed her as a cloud envelops a mountaintop, or covers a valley. Under that sacred covering, God secretly placed the sperm carrying the soul of the Son of God. O wonder of wonders! A sinful woman receives the sinless seed that sanctifies the product of her womb and conceives the soul of the God/man.

Additional verses on virgin conception

• **"But when the fulness of the time was come, God sent forth his Son, <u>made of a woman</u>..."** *(Galatians 4:4).* The Bible clearly states that Jesus was **made of a woman**, that is, he became a fetus in the womb of a woman and developed naturally.

• **"Which <u>were born</u>, not of blood, nor of the will of the flesh, nor of the will of man, <u>but of God</u>. And the Word was <u>made flesh</u>, and dwelt among us, (and we beheld his glory, the glory as of the only begotten of the Father,) full of grace and** truth" (*John 1:13-14*). The preexistent Word was **made flesh** by natural processes.

• **"Concerning his Son Jesus Christ our Lord, which was <u>made</u> of the <u>seed of David</u> according to <u>the flesh</u>"** *(Romans 1:3)*. The emphasis here is that Jesus was **made** to be of the **seed** of David, thus qualifying him for the throne of David in fulfillment of prophecy.

• **"And I will put enmity between thee and the woman, and between thy seed and <u>her seed</u>; it shall bruise thy head, and thou shalt bruise his heel"** *(Genesis 3:15)*. Jesus is called the **seed** of the woman—the product of her womb.

Looking at all the above verses together, it is clear that God is quite comfortable with the idea of sexual reproduction.

Why write something so embarrassing?

It may be embarrassing to you, but not to most of the world—certainly not to this author. I will ask you a question: Why avoid discussing the most important subject to mankind? Wouldn't that be strange, as if God were embarrassed to address that which he had created? Should we surrender this glorious part of God's creation to the devil's dirty domain? Although it is true that Christian ministers and writers tend to avoid this subject, it is time to take back this lost sacred ground.

Sex for reproduction only?

Erotic pleasure came from the brilliant, creative, and

pure mind of a holy God. God created us for his pleasure, and he created sex for our pleasure. Some guilty soul with a twisted religious mind has said that sex is only for procreation and not for pleasure. If that were the case, what was God's purpose when he installed this powerful drive in his creation? Surely he could have made reproduction a lot less complicated. With no pleasure or passion involved, there would never be any fornication, unwed mothers, or broken marriages. When a couple wanted children, they could have burdened themselves to perform some dull fertilization ritual with cold deliberation and forethought.

It is common among some Amish and plain people to believe that sex is for the purpose of reproduction only. I never will forget the time one old fellow cornered me and warned against sex other than to produce children. He proudly testified that he had dutifully abstained after his wife had passed the age of child bearing. I had previously wondered why they fought so vigorously. He was obviously carrying a load or dumping it where he shouldn't—which left him anything but mellow.

Needless to say, I laughed at his ridiculous belief and bragged about my ongoing abilities. I later discovered that their marriage was "forced" due to her pregnancy. His doctrine was supported by his guilt.

Many people seem to think that God indeed invented the tools, but the devil made them fun. Someone said it this way: "God made us English, but the devil made us French."

God has seen fit to inspire eight whole chapters of erotic desire and fulfillment for his people to read, yet he included nothing in this song about having children. Their minds were on personal pleasure— smelling, touching, and tasting one another!

Sex is no more sinful than is talking. Sure, **the tongue is a world of iniquity, setting on fire the course of nature, and who can tame it?** which is simply to draw our attention to the misuse of a thing, not to its inherent nature.

Exhortation to pleasure

The concept that sex is only acceptable when seeking to have children is rooted in the idea that sexual pleasure is evil. It is common to hear someone describe a great pleasure as, "sinfully delicious." This comes from the assumption that if it is wonderfully pleasurable, it must be sinful. The general conviction is that righteousness is dull. Wherever this attitude prevails, someone has allowed the Evil One to define the issues.

True sexual pleasure (designed by God), while being highly pleasurable, is the opposite of selfish, for it is in the act of giving pleasure to another that one ascends to ultimate personal pleasure.

Granted, if sex is reduced to self-stimulation, a kind of extension of masturbation, then one would feel—and should feel—that it is dirty. But a married couple in love, abandoned to the simplicity of natural desires, seeking to gratify the other, is righteousness par excellence.

Proverbs 5:15-19
**15 "<u>Drink waters out of thine own cistern</u>, and running waters out of thine own well.
16 Let thy fountains be dispersed abroad, and rivers of waters in the streets.
17 Let them be only thine own, and not strangers' with thee.** *[He builds on an analogy comparing one's spouse to a private fountain.]*
**18 Let <u>thy fountain be blessed</u>: and rejoice with the wife of thy youth.
19 Let her be as the loving hind and pleasant roe; let <u>her breasts satisfy thee at all times</u>; and be thou <u>ravished always with her love</u>."**

The text encourages the man to **drink** from the body of his wife as he drinks from the sweet waters of his private well. The woman was compared to a cistern or well of water (both of which are closed and still); so when verse 18 says **"Let thy fountain be blessed,"** (a fountain is gushing water) it must be imagery for the discharge of the man. The text is an exhortation to a monogamous relationship.

This word for **ravished** (v. 19) in the original languages is most often used in a negative context. It has to do with being carried away, consumed to distraction, a powerful appetite that possesses the soul. God commands a man to be carried away with passion for the body of his wife.

God commands: **"Live joyfully with the wife whom thou lovest all the days of the life of thy vanity, which he hath given thee under the sun, all the days of thy vanity: for that is thy portion in this life** *[That is what God appointed us to]*, **and in** thy labour which thou takest under the sun" *(Ecclesiastes 9:9).* He acknowledges that life in the flesh is all vanity, for everything that goes back to dust and is not part of eternity is ultimately vanity. But he assures his readers that God has given us a **portion** to be joyfully indulged in during this vain life—one man and one woman in loving embrace.

"**Nevertheless, to avoid fornication, let every man have his own wife, and let every woman have her own husband**" *(1 Corinthians. 7:2).* This passage recognizes the strength of the sex drive and assumes that it is legitimate to seek marriage and the nuptial privileges it offers as a way to avoid fornication.

"**Let the husband <u>render unto the wife due benevolence</u>: and likewise also <u>the wife unto the husband</u>**" *(1 Corinthians 7:3).* It is called *benevolence* to give sexual satisfaction to one's spouse.

"**The wife hath not power of her own body, but the husband: and likewise also the husband hath not power of his own body, but the wife**" *(1 Corinthians 7:4).* One who is married has given his or her body to the other, and does not have the right to withhold it.

"**Defraud ye not one the other...** *[To withhold sexual satisfaction from one's partner is to defraud]* **...except it be with consent for a time, that ye may give yourselves to fasting and prayer; and come together again, that Satan tempt you not for your incontinency**" *(1 Corinthians 7:5).* Again, the assumption is that when one does not have his or her sexual needs met in the marriage, it leaves them open to be tempted of Satan. God intended for a spouse to give more than passive submission. If a woman or a man is not an active and interested participant, they are defrauding their partner.

When Sarah, the wife of Abraham, was very old and many years past the childbearing age, an angel came to visit and informed them that Sarah was going to become pregnant by her husband. She laughed and said, **"shall I have pleasure, my lord being old also?** *(Genesis 18:12).* Sarah's spontaneous response to the announcement was to consider the *pleasure* that such a renewal of her female abilities would bring.

This kind of attitude ran in the family, for, years later, their son Isaac got caught in an outdoor romp. Abimelech, king of the Philistines, looked out his window and saw Isaac and Rebekah **sporting** in the garden, whereupon he surmised that they were married *(Genesis 26:8-9).*

Erotic pleasure is created in the image of worship

God patterned everything he created after his own nature, including all aspects of erotic pleasure and reproduction. For the Bible tells us that by observing creation, we can gain knowledge of the Creator *(Romans 1).* All that is material and finite was created in the image of his non-material self. By attentive searching, we can discover the association of each thing God created with some aspect of his image.

Time, with its past, present, and future, was created in the image of his infinity. Matter was created to
reflect the very existence of God. He created energy
in the image of his power, vast space in the image of
his boundlessness, motion in the image of his activity.
The mind was created in the image of God's wisdom,
the will in the image of his self-determination. The
human body was created in the image of God's connection with physical creation. Music was created in
the image of God's soul. Color was created in the
image of his beauty. The senses of sight, touch, smell,
taste, and hearing were created in the image of God's
experience of himself. The gift of speech and writing
was created in the image of the second person of the
Godhead—the "Word." The human spirit was created
in the image of God's Holy Spirit. Sex, where body,
soul, and spirit merge into oneness, was created in the
image of communion within the Godhead. Erotic
pleasure was created in the image of worship.
Copulation, conception, and birth were created in the
image of God's creative powers.

Anyone who has experienced both the height of
pure spiritual worship and pure erotic pleasure, knows
that one is the image and the other is the reality. Even
if you have never dared consider it, now that it is
brought to your attention, you must know that it is so.

The heights of worship transcend erotic pleasure
in degree, but not kind. Pure worship occurs when one
loses consciousness of self and focuses upon the
person of God with wonder, humility, admiration,
love, and devotion. The state of worship is the most

intense period of concentration one can know. It is almost an out-of-body experience—certainly out of this world. It is the height of purity, wholeness, peace, joy, and love. It is a state of being from which one never wants to leave.

If you still haven't come to accept my stated conclusion, then tell me, what <u>did</u> God create that is in the image of worship, if not erotic pleasure? And what then does erotic pleasure reflect of God's nature? What does its very prominence on the pages of Scripture and in the physiology of the human race say about the Creator who designed it?

The Song of Solomon exalts erotic desire and fulfillment to a plane that has led most commentators to conclude that it must necessarily be an analogy of love between Christ and his church. Have they not seen the very reality the Holy Scriptures have so plainly stated? It must be that writers rush so quickly to the spiritual plane that they fail to draw their reader's attention to the plain sense of the text. If I appear bolder than others, nonetheless, I stand on historical ground in my interpretation of this song. If the many commentators are correct in viewing this as a picture of Christ and his church, then consider that it was God who chose and carefully crafted an erotic song to represent worship.

If the only worship you have experienced has been ritualistic and structured, or if the only sex you have experienced is selfish and dirty, you will not be able to understand the analogy of erotic pleasure to worship, which God so clearly "pictures" in his inspired word. If this is the case with you, don't be discouraged; there is a way of cleansing and recovery, which we will come to shortly.

Objection that the song is not meant to be a discussion of sex

If this was not meant to be a discussion of sexual pleasure, the author of the song should have flunked his writing class. Why seduce your audience with clear images of erotic pleasure if you want to lead their minds to something entirely different? If we should say, as do others, that this erotic description is meant to be an analogy of Christ and the church, we have not weakened the erotic content of this book; rather, we have elevated it to the dignity and holiness of that which it typifies. One chooses an analogy for two reasons: first, its similarity to the thing it is to depict, and second, its familiarity to the audience. The reader cannot draw the parallel unless he first thinks upon the typical. If you object to considering the sexual content of the Song of Solomon as important and practical for all married couples, you, of all people, need it most. Have you ever wondered why you don't smile as much as some of us do?

The association of smell and taste with the sex drive

It is clear from several passages that the author of this song speaks metaphorically of the bodies of the main actors as fruit, flowers, wine, aromatic herbs, spices, honeycomb, milk, and fountains of waters to be consumed. Their nostrils are filled with odors of each other, and everything pleasant they experience through their senses reminds them of the love they share.

He compares her **breasts to clusters** *of grapes,* and says the **"smell of thy nose** *[is]* **like apples; And the roof of thy mouth like the best wine"** *(Song of Solomon 7:7-9).*

She says of him**, "Thy lips, O my spouse, drop as the honeycomb: honey and milk are under thy tongue; and the smell of thy garments is like the smell of Lebanon"** *(Song of Solomon 4:11).* Out of a desire to taste him deeply, she explores the inside of his mouth with her tongue, comparing the taste of his mouth to *honey* and *milk.*

In 4:11-5:1 he compares her to a garden of sweet fruit and spices, and she responds by calling upon the gentle cool breezes to blow upon her fruit until **the spices flow out.** He then is attracted to the flowing juices of her body and comes to drink and eat.

Science has established the organic link between pleasant odors and sexual drive. But before science ever came along, every young male could tell you that when he smelled gardenias or honeysuckle, he thought of some lovely female in his life or of the one in his dreams. Why do young men bring flowers and candy? Why do young ladies anoint themselves with sensual odors? Why do couples eat by candlelight with flowers in the center of the table? Because smell and taste are stimuli to the sexual drive.

The book of Proverbs gives an account of a woman attempting to seduce a man into a sexual encounter with these words: **"I have perfumed my**

bed with myrrh, aloes, and cinnamon. Come, let us
take our fill of love until the morning: let us solace
ourselves with loves" *(Proverbs 7:17-18)*.

Scientific studies have revealed that natural body
odors are more seductive than the most expensive
chemical perfumes. After that, domestic spices like
cinnamon have proven to be highly stimulating. Take
an apple pie to bed and...well...look out!

As strange as it seems, clinical studies have
proven that artificial perfumes actually diminish the
sex drive. The clinicians jokingly call commercial
perfumes "pesticides." However, a man or woman can
be conditioned to identify the odors of gaudy
perfumes with erotic experiences, but it must be a
learned response—a taste this author never acquired.

If you want to cut through all the cultural
conditioning and get back to natural responses, there
is no odor so intoxicating as the pure, natural odor of
your spouse, and no taste so sweet as the head-to-toe
delicacy of your God-given mate. Many a lover has
said to his or her mate, "You look so good, I could eat
you," and then proceeded to do just that.

If you have a hang-up about sex, you didn't get it
from the Holy Spirit; you got it from a world that has
never learned to handle something so wonderful and
powerful as pure, heavenly, eroticism. When is the
last time you, like the lady in our song, washed
yourself, anointed your body or your bed with
stimulating, natural odors, ate and drank something
pleasant, dressed provocatively, adjusted the lights,
undressed provocatively, and then "went to heaven?"

God created Adam and Eve, said it was very good, brought the first naked woman to the first naked man, and commanded them to copulate. It is what he gave to the sons of men as their **"portion in this life"** *(Ecclesiastes 9:9)*. He created marriage **"...to be received with thanksgiving of them which believe and know the truth"** *(1 Timothy 4:3)*, **"And whatsoever ye do, do *it* heartily, as to the Lord, and not unto men"** *(Colossians 3:23)*.

What is natural sex? What is perverted?

I have been amazed on several occasions by individuals who ask me how a man could live with his wife and not lust after her. I am always shocked. I know how this twisted outlook comes about, but, given my holy experience, it is always unbelievable to have someone reveal that he thinks marital sexual activity is evil. In our present society, perversion is more common than normalcy.

We will not list and discuss the many forms of perversion. This author, in spite of the fact that he has ministered on the streets and in prisons for 40 years, could not name ten percent of the possible perversions. We can come to our point more directly by discussing that which is natural. Romans 1:26-27 speaks of the **natural use of the woman**. The passage reveals that same-sex activity is **against nature**.

There are married couples who abstain from certain forms of perfectly lawful and natural foreplay for fear that it is unnatural, while there are unbelievers who justify all manner of aberrant perversions, professing that to them it is a natural desire. So how do we determine what is natural to the sexual relationship of a married couple?

God's book on sex doesn't take us very far into the bedroom of this couple. But several things are clear. She dressed and undressed to attract him. She put on natural odors that were seductive, prepared her bed with the same, put on jewelry to attract him, and prepared herself with deep erotic imaginations of him. They delighted in the nakedness of the other, as seen by their joyful description of the beauty of all parts of their bodies. They tasted each other as fruit, and drank of the other as wine and water. He lay all night upon her naked breasts. She admired his thighs, belly, and testicles. He admired her hips and bare belly, seeming to be attracted to her pubic hair. They came together with complete abandonment and joyful passion. It is totally natural for married lovers to taste each other from head to toe. There is something so pure and uncomplicated in their total absorption with each other.

Sexual expression that is good and natural will come to the innocent couple spontaneously. It doesn't need to be taught. Various forms of sexual foreplay and expression are rediscovered with each couple in the normal course of their growth and experimentation.

If your bedroom gets boring, try the trampoline at night, or a lonely hilltop on a windy autumn day. Camping trips can be a trip, and you simply must find a lonely place and skinny-dip together. The kitchen, the carport, the wood-shed or the barn, all are natural and good places. Some of your pleasures will be discussed and planned, and some will be spontaneous, catching both of you by surprise. Just be careful not to surprise the kids, the neighbors, other swimmers, or mountain trail hikers.

Love and commitment only produce what is natural. It is never violent, abusive, or degrading. If a man truly loves a woman, he will approach sex as a way to satisfy her, to elevate her person, to thrill and bless her. Good sex can be quiet and tender one time and rowdy and rambunctious another, but it always leaves one mellow and pure in spirit. It is as clear as spring water and as holy as a prayer meeting.

Baggage

Problems arise when people come to marriage with baggage—hang-ups—or when they have their thinking twisted through exposure to Hollywood, pornography, or deviant behavior learned in the company of others already perverted.

There is a natural threshold of sexual expression that completely satisfies the deepest longings of the human body and soul. Though physical sex is a beautiful form of expression, true satisfaction is ultimately found in the spirit. This is true in every facet of human existence.

But the wicked will never find spiritual satisfaction. Therefore sex never satisfies them. They can satiate their hunger, but they can never rise to true satisfaction. Old forms of expression grow dull, and they must dare to experiment with new and forbidden things that have nothing to do with expressing love.

Here is where the devil has his field day. By coupling degrading or violent acts with the sexual passion, these offensive acts take on the excitement of sex, and in time seem to be a part of it. The more daring and deviant the acts, the greater the thrill. For those people, there comes a time when sex without all the alien trappings ceases to be sex. The powerful appetite for sex becomes the sanctuary and point of entry for all forms of alien behavior. It will be impossible to communicate this concept to a pervert, for his perversion has worked its way upstream until it has polluted the very fountains from which flow his human personality.

I know that many of my readers are waiting for me to list the forms of acceptable and unacceptable foreplay. By way of principle, I will say that any activity that does not spring from love and contribute to love is wrong. Love never involves coercion. It doesn't produce guilt.

It is possible for you to 'feel' guilt that is inappropriate. A misinformed mind, caused by former associations, can come to view the holy as if it were profane. Removing that false guilt is one of the purposes of this study. Your exposure to the Word of God on this subject will automatically begin the process of freeing you from false guilt.

Perversions

As to specifics: the rectum is for waste disposal and is never meant to be part of sexual expression. That is the reason God placed it out of sight, deep in the buttocks. No innocent young couple would ever "discover" the other's rectum or find satisfaction in their own being fondled or penetrated. The idea of rectal penetration came about because queers found it the closest thing to the female vagina. Rectal sex is sodomy, and it is sick. A wife should refuse to participate. A man whose interests lie in that direction should decide whether he wants to be a queer or a husband—one or the other. Men, don't use your wife contrary to nature—and, wives, don't be so used.

All forms of bondage, blood, beating, or inflicting pain are perversions that are learned, not natural desires. Such things are a simulation of rape and violence. Even in their mildest forms, these deviations are fantasies in violence and perversion, the practice or pretense of evil, preparation for crimes worthy of death. The person who desires such things is lost to true love. He will spend eternity in bondage, suffering the fires of Hell. A wife should refuse to participate.

It goes without saying that all sexual activity between same-sex partners is perversion, as is all sexual activity outside of marriage and all adultery and incest. The use of pornography is tantamount to indulging in adultery, fornication, homosexuality, bestiality, incest, child molestation, and every deviant thing it portrays. Pornography is anti-love and hijacks erotic pleasure, elevating it to a place of deity. It is the devil's substitute god, an act of dark worship. It ceases to be sex and becomes an extension of masturbation. One who uses it reminds me of a rabid dog eating himself. If you are participating in one of these perversions, you have divorced God and are courting Hell.

So you were wounded when you were young

It is a common excuse; a wife says, "I don't like sex because I was wounded when I was young. I was abused as a child. I had several ugly experiences." In effect, she is saying, "I am hurt; I am not normal; don't expect me to love and be loved as God intended, for I am broken. Please excuse me from my duties and the opportunity to experience pleasure."

God anticipated your excuse, and so recorded the fact that the lady of this song came from a disadvantaged background, was raised by people who were angry with her, and made fun of her *(1:6)*.

Others have accepted the forgiveness of God, thrown away their bitterness, and acted as God intended. You can, too. The path to healing is to know the truth and then act accordingly, regardless of how you feel. **"Commit thy works unto the LORD, and thy thoughts shall be established"** *(Proverbs 16:3)*.

Guilt

"Every sin that a man doeth is without the body; but he that committeth fornication sinneth against his own body" *(1 Corinthians 6:18)*. This passage puts sexual sin in a category all by itself—sin against one's own body. It leaves a weight on the conscience like nothing else. This is not an abstract doctrine; it is universal experience. Guilt is one word that preachers and psychiatrists never need define for the public.

Experience has proven that no sin has the power to permanently stain the conscience as does sexual sin.

Many bank robbers fleeing the scene with a bag of money have been shocked when the bag suddenly exploded with red dye. All the money and the robber are indelibly stained. At that point the money is rendered unusable and the robber is marked for all to see. Likewise, when young people violate their consciences and steal a little sex, whether it is in the form of pornography, same-sex experimentation, voyeurism, or teenagers "making love," their consciences are permanently stained. Outside of God, the only way to make the stain go away is to gravitate into a world where everyone and everything is stained red. The citizens of such a society learn to be comfortable with the stain and eventually come to deny that red exists.

Though few people live in a world that is all red, most adults are marked with some stain. Many studies report that more than half of all married women, who are capable of doing so, do not come to a climax when they have sex. Counselors reveal that it is very common for married women carrying the baggage of guilt to find sex repugnant, that is, until they are lured into an extramarital affair, at which time they "feel" young again, and it is all so exciting as before. However, when the new wears off and the stain of guilt grows darker, the freeze once more creeps into their bed. Again sex seems dirty, and they are nauseated by it. They do not know the source of their sexual dysfunction. Some turn to pornography, some to alcohol or drugs, others to sex therapy, counseling, or further extramarital affairs. The stain spreads; the soul grows cold; and they take to watching soaps and listening to romantic songs that fantasize of true love.

It is very common for women to say that they become nauseated when they know their husband wants to "do it." Wives reveal how they wait until their husbands are asleep before going to bed, or they rush to bed before he does and pretend to be asleep—anything to avoid sexual activity. Others tell their counselors that they just lie there cooperating, but not participating, and try to think about something else.

This frigid state is most often a result of the guilt they unconsciously associate with sexual activity. In a similar way, when I see an orange and think about eating it, the muscles in my jaw involuntarily constrict. Likewise, when I see a dental chair, I can feel the vibrations in my head. The association of two things occurring at the same time conditions the person to view them as one and the same—an orange and constricting jaw muscles, dental chairs and vibrations, sex and shame.

When I was a child, I loved chocolate-covered cherries. Nothing in the world could compare. But on one occasion when I had spent the previous week in bed with the flu, someone gave this sick boy a whole box of chocolate-covered cherries. I had never eaten more than one or two cherries at a time. This was an indulgence of preposterous proportions. I ate half the box before I began to throw up the soured, acidy syrup. To this day when I see a chocolate-covered cherry, I am nauseated. I will eat one if you make me, but it is not pleasant. I like cherries, and I like chocolate, but I am conditioned now to sincerely feel that chocolate-covered cherries are 'sinful.' Just one experience is all it took. I know that I have an unreasonable phobia. I am now fifty-six years old, and it makes me sick to write about it. For fifty years I have been controlled by that one negative conditioning experience.

In a similar manner—though on a different level—a person can be induced to associate sex with guilt and sin. It happens like this: A young girl knows she should not engage in sex before marriage, but she is overcome with passion; so she sneaks around like a thief and violates her conscience. Later, she feels guilty and tells herself that she will not be a "bad girl" again. But in time, passion overrides the conscience, and she once again succumbs to the temptation.

Two things are happening at the same time: She is feeling guilty, and she is having sex. Sex and guilt become synonymous in her subconscious mind. But while "love" is young, the passion is still stronger than the guilt. Yet there comes a time, after she is married and the passions of sex have been satisfied, that guilt will come to the surface and be stronger than the passion. The guilt and shame will shut down her sexual responses, and she will view her husband's advances as I view chocolate-covered cherries— something to be regurgitated. The more often guilt and shame smother her sexual responses, the stronger grows the shame and her inability to respond to his advances. She will grow into a confirmed state of frigidity.

Now you know the rest of the story. You weren't born broken. You broke yourself.

Most men respond to guilt differently. Rather than freezing up and withdrawing, they become demanding and aggressive. They seek more sex more often, and it takes on the form of dominance and exploitation, rather than sharing and loving. They cease to care for the ladies, but continue to use them as a 'necessary evil.' In extreme cases, guilty men take out their feelings of self-condemnation by punishing the objects of their lust. That is how the "F" word came to be used as an aggressive, threatening curse. The man who uses it, uses women and views sex as an act of dominance and violence.

The world of sexual exploitation and guilt is a dark pit where the sex drive no longer resembles the marvelous vehicle of passion God created. It is a vortex spiraling downward into the fires of lust and hell. For many, there is no return. The lower you descend, the less likely you will ever believe there is any other way. The Garden of Eden gives place to the whorehouse of horrors. Paradise turns to pain. What God wondrously created, the devil commandeers, and the end does not resemble the beginning.

But God is not ready to surrender his blessed gift of marital love to the manipulations of Satan. He is ready to forgive and restore. His redemption can accomplish that which no psychiatrist or sex counselor ever dared dream.

Overcoming guilt associations

The two examples of conditioning that I gave (the orange and the chocolate-covered cherries) are minor compared to guilt conditioning. As we discussed, when two things that are not necessarily related happen at the same time, the soul can be conditioned to accept a permanent association. But the guilt that haunts a person in respect to past, sinful, sexual acts is more than mere conditioning, for there is a direct relationship between sinful acts and ongoing guilt. In fact, the guilt is appropriate—even necessary to our happiness.

Knowing that guilt prevents us from functioning normally, you will wonder how I can say that it is beneficial. Think about it. If you did not suffer guilt, you would go on in your sin, unaware that it was leading you in a destructive direction. Guilt is the pain of the soul, the warning that you are endangering your person. In most cases, guilt speaks the truth. Without guilt, we would live like animals, follow our passions, and ignore our brains; but our moral natures will not allow us to live without the voice of conscience.

Guilt doesn't just go away with the years. The soul is not equipped, as is the body, to heal itself from sin. Only God can heal the soul from sin. Even after you have put sin behind you, painful guilt clings to your soul, crying for forgiveness. You cannot forgive yourself. You must go to your Maker whom you have offended. It is his world you live in. It was with one of his creatures that you violated the laws of your nature. It is his air that you breathe, and he holds the keys to eternity. There is a heaven, and there is a hell. Guilt remains to warn you that *The Judge of all the earth* has not forgotten. Heaven holds your records in anticipation of the day when you will be forced to appear before the judgment and give account of every deed you have ever done. Guilt warns the indifferent soul that, "He has not forgotten." Go to your Creator and Savior while there is still time. Receive the forgiveness he so freely offers. Only he can remove your guilt and restore your soul. Then you can enjoy all things, including sex, as God intended.

God didn't make us to feel guilt as a form of punishment. The purpose of guilt is to drive us back to himself. When guilt says, "You are unworthy; you deserve to be punished," it speaks the truth.

Goodbye, Guilt

But the good news is that God sent his own son, Jesus, into the world to take the place of guilty sinners. Jesus never sinned. He felt no guilt. His conscience was clear before God. Since Adam, there has never been another man like Jesus who did all things pleasing to God. In every way, at all times, without exception, he pleased the Father, whereas we have displeased him.

Yet Jesus did not come just to give us an example. He came to be our substitute—to take the place of us sinners and bear the punishment for all our sin. At the end of his righteous life, he voluntarily died, as if he were the sinner. He took your sin upon himself and died in your place—in the place of all sinners. Forgiveness does not come through the church or through its leaders. Only God can forgive, and he is ready to forgive all who will believe and receive his forgiveness.

"If we confess our sins, he is faithful and just to forgive us our sins, and to cleanse us from all

unrighteousness" *(1 John 1:9).*

His forgiveness for you is not measured by your forgiveness of yourself. He forgives even when your conscience is condemning you. It is only after you believe that he has forgiven you that you will be free from guilt. In a short time, as you walk in fellowship with Jesus, the pain and memory of your past sins will fade and you will see a slow change occurring.

Just as quickly as the conscience will condemn immoral behavior, it will approve righteous behavior. You have now read many verses that express God's attitude toward sex. This one summarizes it very well: **"Marriage is honourable in all, and the <u>bed undefiled</u>: but whoremongers and adulterers God will judge"** *(Hebrews 13:4).*

Practical advice

You may say, "But it has been many years since I sinned. I confessed it to God, and I know that he forgave me, but I developed this permanent hang-up. How can I make my subconscious mind accept what my conscious mind knows?" I told you of my experience with chocolate-covered cherries. I now know that the candy did not make me sick, and that if I ate it today it would not harm me, but I am conditioned to associate chocolate-covered cherries with regurgitation. If I felt that it was needful for me to overcome my mental block, I would not sit around waiting for my twisted thinking to go away. I would force myself to eat the threatening food until I reprogrammed my mind with pleasant experiences. If I were to eat the candy a few times and enjoy it, the new experiences would become the standard. As it is, every time I refuse chocolate-covered cherries, I confirm the old thought patterns and perpetuate the misconception.

God removes the guilt, something you cannot do. <u>But you must take the steps to reprogram your responses</u>. If you are a woman, you may need to overcome your coldness toward sex. If you are a man, you may need to overcome your lack of sensitivity. Both can be overcome by approaching lovemaking in a pure and holy way. It will take time, but you *can* reprogram your human responses through several good experiences. And it will be more than worth the effort!

The key is to not wait for some inner signal that everything is all right. Determine to act in a manner that will bless your spouse. Act in a loving way. <u>Do what you ought to do because it is good for the other person.</u> Love is in the doing, not the feelings. <u>If you 'do' love, in time you will 'feel' love.</u> If you surrender your body to your mate for your mate's pleasure, you will come to enjoy it yourself.

Romance and spiritualism

On several occasions when women have explained their coldness toward sex by saying that they want their husbands to be sensitive and spiritual, my wife has responded, "What do you want him to do, sing hallelujah while you are doing it?" The first time I heard her answer a woman that way, I said, "Sometimes I feel like singing hallelujah, but I don't want to disturb the kids."

Women are different from men in that regard.
They need romance and emotional bonding. When a
husband seeks to be close sexually, but not
emotionally and spiritually, a woman will feel that
their intimacy is not anything above animal instinct.
And, unfortunately, that is often the case. Not that
there is anything wrong with the animal drive, but we
are created to be more than a body of drives. We are
also living souls, created in God's image, and that part
of us must find expression as well.

I would counsel the man to meet his wife's needs.
Learn to care in more ways than just physical. Value
the soul of your wife, and give her the romance she
needs. The doing of it will fulfill a need in you as
well.

And I would counsel the wife to recognize that her
husband may never be different. Some men are so
insensitive that the only affection they ever show is
through physical sex. That being the case, if a wife
should be resistant to her husband by holding out until
he meets her spiritual or social needs, there will never
be any resolution. If she were to accept his
shortcoming and respond sexually, there is a better
chance that through sex he will come to love her in a
deeper way. If not, then the woman will still benefit
by enjoying sex herself. Why deprive yourself just to
prove a point that may never be appreciated?

Drink abundantly

When Deb and I first got married, we had occasional

fights. She was trying to change me, and I was trying to change her. One day she was complaining to an older woman about my stubbornness. The older woman suggested that Deb just "hold out" on me. "That will bring him around," the woman said. When Deb told me how she responded to the woman, it became my all-time favorite quote. Upon hearing the woman's suggestion, Deb looked shocked and, after a moment of contemplation, said, "But that would hurt me as much as it would him!" I love it! I love her. We don't fight any more. As the old song says, "It's lovin' in the morning, lovin' in the evening, and lovin' when the sun goes down."

When I called Deb into my office to read the above paragraph, she laughed and said, "Huh! The men will know better. It is "wishin' in the morning, wishin' in the evening, and MAYBE when the sun goes down." I told her, "I meant before we turned fifty. So…maybe we skip a day now and then."

On several occasions when I have heard women say, "All men think about is sex," I have assured them that this was not the case at all. Sex is not the only thing men think about. Afterward they think about sleeping, and when they wake up, they think about eating. If you can't laugh and enjoy erotic pleasure, you are tied in one knot too many.

You are human and you are flesh—as God intended. If you have not been enjoying the gift God gave to you—your spouse—it is high time you did; it is not too late. I remind you of the exhortation Solomon gave his readers in 5:1, **"O friends; drink, yea, drink abundantly."** And by now, you know he was not talking about water.

Multifaceted being

Sex is the most powerful and wonderful blessing God
gave to man. For that reason the mechanics of it can
be made to stand alone. It can be wrenched from its
intended context and used independently until it
becomes the user. Like releasing a hungry bear from
its cage, it can turn and consume you. It can take the
place of the Creator who gave it. If allowed to run
wild and follow its own course, it can take the place
of the personality itself. Like all things God made, it
is meant to be managed, to be harnessed, directed, and
disciplined.

We humans are created to be multifaceted beings,
a delicate balance of many attributes, especially of the
flesh and the spirit. The human personality is
inadequate to reach its potential alone. It is because
our original ancestor disobeyed God and separated
both himself and all his posterity from fellowship with
God, that appetites originally meant to exist in
balance now dominate the human race.

Because of the strength of appetite, even the most
tranquil and philosophical soul is unable to maintain
the balance of his nature. History is a chronicle of that
failure. Philosophy and religion are testimony to the
confusion and uncertainty of the most noble among
us. War, rape, sexual perversions, and divorce are
proof that there is a disconnect somewhere. Until the
connection is made back to God through Jesus Christ,
the greatest blessing will continue to be the greatest
curse—producing more heartache and destruction to

the human race than all other appetites combined.

Fading remnants of glory remain in all humans.
Most people are content to be made captive by their
appetites, gaining what enjoyment they can along the
way. But the righteous—those who have been born-
again into the family and fellowship of God, those
who walk in subjection to the Holy Spirit and bring
their bodies under his discipline—are able to live in
the glory others only dream about. As we serve God,
our appetites serve us instead of driving us, and both
body and soul, now in harmony, experience the
fullness of all earthly pleasures—including the erotic.
Man was created to be holy in all things. Thank God
for holy sex!

The summit

If our lives were music, sex would be the crescendo.
The musical piece has many gentle and soothing
moments, but it builds to a dynamic climax when
every instrument joins together to celebrate the entire
evening. Applause follows, and the musicians are left
drained, but satisfied. Likewise, foreplay and
copulation are the satisfactory conclusions to the
experiences of two people living daily in harmony.
Without the song, the crescendo would mean little, for
it would be out of context.

Or, to say it another way, just like the last few
steps that bring a mountain climber to the summit,
erotic love is best when it is the pinnacle of an
extended experience of love. Sex may seem to be the
destination, but it is made rich by the trip. It is just the
final ascent of intimate love that has been shared

during the climb. Without the climb, reaching the
summit would be just another road-side stop. In other
words, sex is not the whole; it is the ultimate
satisfactory conclusion to a great climb, the summit of
oneness, when a couple merges into the highest
communion known to mortals.

To say it in everyday language, copulation is not
the whole party; it is just the fireworks. Fireworks
alone may come to be obnoxious, intrusive, and
spiritually unsatisfying. The bang is best when it is
the celebration of something in the spirit.

I am not trying to make a distinction between
foreplay and copulation, unless by foreplay we are
referring to every moment between summits and we
are including the spirit and soul in the foreplay.

Nor am I suggesting that sex between married
couples is wrong unless it is done in a certain spiritual
context. The animal passion of sex is to be received
with thanksgiving, but we are more than animals; and
if we would be all that our Creator intended, there are
other areas of our being that must be satisfied. Sex is
obviously an act of the body to the gratifying of the
flesh. But it is best when it is also an act of the soul
and spirit. The merging of bodies satisfies our God-
given "itch," but the merging of souls satisfies our
God-given spirits.

When love is more than sex, sex is more than you
could ever imagine. A man should first love his wife
in the same way that he loves his mother, his children,
and his dearest friends. There is nothing erotic in that
kind of love, but it is deep, unselfish, and pure. You

take your infant daughter into your arms, and you inhale her odor; you taste her skin with a light kiss; you hold her tightly, promising to always protect her and be there in time of need. You love till it hurts. You would give your life for that child. Her soul is precious to you.

Men, if you first love the soul of your wife, your love for her body will be well received. Before she feels any sexual passion, your wife will melt under your caring stare. She will long for your massaging touch, and she will willingly yield her body to be tasted and fondled. After having loved someone to distraction—till it hurts—desiring to merge into oneness and stay there forever, the most unimaginable pleasure occurs, and the two rise to the summit to become one.

God made provision for the couple to go beyond the vail, into the holy, intimate place, where none but the two of them can ever go. They return to Eden and perhaps visit a "bit of heaven," and when it is over, their ache for love has been transformed into the purest satisfaction. The two of them are content that they have expressed their love to the fullest. They have become one flesh. God has joined them together. The physical and the spiritual met together and found equilibrium. The two of them can then go out and whip the world together. They are a team. They are one. Forever.

I will be personal for a moment. When I was young and my wife was fresh with the pink, moist passion of youth, the animal ran strong. I loved her, but not as I do today when we are in our fifties. When

we were in our twenties, I never considered that erotic
pleasure might be anything more than a fun necessity.
I knew nothing of the richness that was growing in
our spirits. I had no idea that love could ever be
anything more than dynamite and lightning. But after
more than thirty years, my marriage has caught up
with my spirituality. I now have a marriage that is
proof of the existence of God. I am never so human as
in marriage and yet never more close to the divine.

As we age, our passions fade, but our spirits soar.
I envision a time—if we live to be old—when the
tired animal lies quietly by the hearth while our spirits
climb the last few paces to the summit. We may look
back and laugh at the vigor we once knew, of
passionate fires long since burnt out, but we will not
look back in regret, and there will be no sense of loss,
for even now the wonderful, glorious flesh has been
exceeded by a merging of spirits until the unseen is
far more tangible than the seen. As our bodies sag and
creak, as the flesh breaks down and leans over to face
the cold ground, there has been a life kindled that
burns more in the spirit world than in the bedroom. If
my wife faded away until nothing was left but her
spirit, I would put that dear spirit in a bottle and
inhale it until my last breath. **Praise God for his
wonderful works to children of men.**

By the way, I am not that old yet. I feel the fuse
burning even now. Lightning will strike before the
day is ended.

Postscript

Even now, before anyone has read this little book, I

know that there are some who will misunderstand and misapply the things I have said. There are always those whose bitterness, self-pity, or anger are so deep and precious to them that they filter out all information but that which supports their crippled perspective.

A few men will use small portions of this material to justify their twisted, carnal world-view. They will go on using women as nothing more than a support team for their self-love—as dumps for their semen. Their souls will grow smaller until they are horribly alone, loving nothing but their fantasies. The wages of sin is death—loneliness, bitterness, grief, regret, and, most of all, emptiness. Passions will fade and the body will die; the spirit will stand alone, dressed in the garment it wove in this life. Eternity will be an orgasm of holiness and love, but these folks will not be welcomed. I cannot help them now. And God will not help them then.

I am especially concerned for the many women whom I know will respond to these words inappropriately. If you are one of whom I speak, you have tunnel vision. Throughout the reading of this book and even now, you are thinking, "If only my husband loved me as you love your wife, I would gladly yield to him and be an eager sex partner." Every day Deb and I read letters from women who explain their poor marriages with statements like, "If my husband loved me as Christ loves the church...." There are many ways women have said it, but it all means, "I will not be a happy person or a good sex partner until my husband earns my love and devotion." Well, lady, you get one last kiss. You can kiss happiness goodbye. God will give you salvation, but he doesn't GIVE anyone a good marriage. You work for it. You sacrifice. Until you determine to be a good wife, even when you are not treated so, your marriage will never grow. Marriages grow as people grow. You cannot make a better marriage by waiting for the other half to improve. Don't wait for marriage to make you a better wife and person. It will never happen. If you become the better person, your marriage will improve.

Here is the key. You must determine that, for the glory of God, you will be the kind of wife you should be even if it never changes your husband.

Let me say it plainly. Give your husband pleasure when he doesn't deserve it. Minister to him in every way—including sex. Treat erotic pleasure as your royal duty. If you wait until everything is right spiritually before you participate in the flesh, it will NEVER happen.

Finally, I will say it one more time. Do you want a better marriage? Fine, so does your spouse. Now go practice Christian love. Give your partner a better marriage and forget about yourself. That is the essence of love—any kind of love.

Philippians 2:3-8
3 Let nothing be done through strife or vainglory; but in lowliness of mind let **each esteem other better than themselves**.
4 Look **not every man on his own things,** but every man also on the things of others.
5 Let this mind be in you, which was also in

Christ Jesus:
6 Who, being in the form of God, thought it not
robbery to be equal with God:
**7 But made himself of no reputation, and took
upon him the form of a servant**, and was made
in the likeness of men:
8 And being found in fashion as a man, **he
humbled himself, and became obedient** unto
death, even the death of the cross.

There is no life so rich, no pleasure so thorough,
as that of a holy Christian. Humanity reaches its
highest expression when in fellowship with Jesus
Christ. You know the way. Now go thou and do
likewise.

FREE *Magazine Subscription*

No Greater Joy Ministries Inc. publishes a bimonthly magazine with answers to questions received in the mail. Send us your name and mailing address and we will put you on our mailing list. Your information is confidential. We do not share your information with anyone.

If you are on our mailing list, you will also receive notification of when the Pearls are speaking in your area. You can also read additional material on our website www.nogreaterjoy.org or you can sign up on our website to receive No Greater Joy.

Write today and receive a free subscription to our magazine!

No Greater Joy Ministries Inc.
1000 Pearl Road
Pleasantville TN 37033
United States of America

www.NoGreaterJoy.org

Other books
by *Michael Pearl*

To Train Up A Child
No Greater Joy Vol. 1
No Greater Joy Vol. 2
No Greater Joy Vol. 3
Romans - Commentary
By Divine Design
Repentance
To Betroth or Not to Betroth
Pornography–Road to Hell
Baptism in Jesus' Name
In Defense of *Biblical*
Chastisement

No Greater Joy Ministries Inc.
1000 Pearl Road
Pleasantville TN 37033
United States of America

www.NoGreaterJoy.org